I0813564

SPORTS SUPERSTARS

RUSSELL WESTBROOK

By Kevin Frederickson

Kaleidoscope
Minneapolis, MN

Your Front Row Seat to the Games

This edition is co-published by agreement between Kaleidoscope and World Book, Inc.

Kaleidoscope Publishing, Inc.
6012 Blue Circle Drive
Minnetonka, MN 55343 U.S.A.

World Book, Inc.
180 North LaSalle St., Suite 900
Chicago IL 60601 U.S.A.

Kaleidoscope ISBNs
978-1-64519-046-2 (library bound)
978-1-64494-203-1 (paperback)
978-1-64519-147-6 (ebook)

World Book ISBN
978-0-7166-4350-0 (library bound)

Library of Congress Control Number
2019940065

Printed in the United States of America.

TABLE OF CONTENTS

CHAPTER 1

Triple Threat

The ball bounces off the rim. Shoes squeak on the court. Players run to the ball. Russell Westbrook watches. He is surrounded by taller players. But no matter. Westbrook knows he can beat them.

He leaps up. He tips the ball back toward the basket. It drops through. Westbrook is 6-foot-3 (1.91 m). That is shorter than many players. But it doesn't stop him from being a star.

This April 2017 game is important. His Oklahoma City Thunder are playing the Denver Nuggets. Westbrook can break a National Basketball Association (NBA) record. It is for most **triple-doubles** in one season.

FUN FACT
The average NBA player is about 6-foot-7 (2 m)!

Russell Westbrook is not the tallest player on the court, but he brings skill and passion to his game.

Westbrook is known not just for scoring, but also for passing to help out teammates.

Westbrook handles the ball in the second quarter. He dribbles just inside the three-point line. He fires up a shot. Westbrook starts running back. He knows it's going in. Swish! Westbrook is confident. He backs it up on the court.

Now it's the fourth quarter. Westbrook looks to the right corner. Just a few minutes remain. He sees Semaj Christon open. Westbrook fires a pass. Christon throws up a three-point shot. It's good! It is Westbrook's tenth **assist** of the game. That gives him a triple-double. It is his 42nd of the season. That is a new record.

Westbrook still has more in him. Oklahoma City trails 105–103. Only three seconds are left. Thunder teammate Steven Adams gets the ball. He passes to Westbrook. Westbrook jumps up. He launches a three-point shot. The ball rings through the hoop. The buzzer sounds! The Thunder win 106–105.

Westbrook jumps in the air. His teammates run over to celebrate. Westbrook finished the game with 50 points. He added 16 rebounds and 10 assists. Westbrook helped turn the Thunder into a great team. Doing that took a lot of hard work.

Westbrook celebrates with teammates after winning the game and setting a new record.

CAREER STATS

Through the 2018–19 season

POINTS PER GAME	23.0
REBOUNDS PER GAME	7.0
ASSISTS PER GAME	8.4
CAREER POINTS	18,859
THREE-POINT ACCURACY	30.8%

CHAPTER 2

California Dreaming

Russell Westbrook stood in the park with his dad. Russell was taking shots. He did it over and over. Then it was time to work out. He did push-ups. He did pull-ups. And he did sit-ups.

Russell was born on November 12, 1988. He grew up near Los Angeles, California. He loved basketball as a kid. He spent hours playing with his dad and friends.

Many players get their start playing on public courts with their parents or friends.

Westbrook pays tribute to his friend with a bracelet. He wears it when he arrives on the court for warm-ups and stretching.

Khelcey Barrs was Russell's best friend. The two spent many hours playing basketball. They played together in **pickup** games. They wanted to play together in high school and college.

One day, Khelcey was playing pickup basketball. He fell on the floor. Players thought he was joking. But Khelcey had a heart condition. He didn't even know about it. He died at age 16. Russell still remembers his friend. He wears a bracelet that says "KB3."

College coaches didn't look at Russell right away. He was 5-foot-8 (1.73 m). He weighed 140 pounds (64 kg). But then he grew. Russell was taller and heavier. Then the University of California, Los Angeles (UCLA) saw him play. And they wanted him. UCLA was the school of Russell's dreams.

FUN FACT

Russell grew five inches (12.7 cm) between his junior and senior seasons.

Where Westbrook Has Been

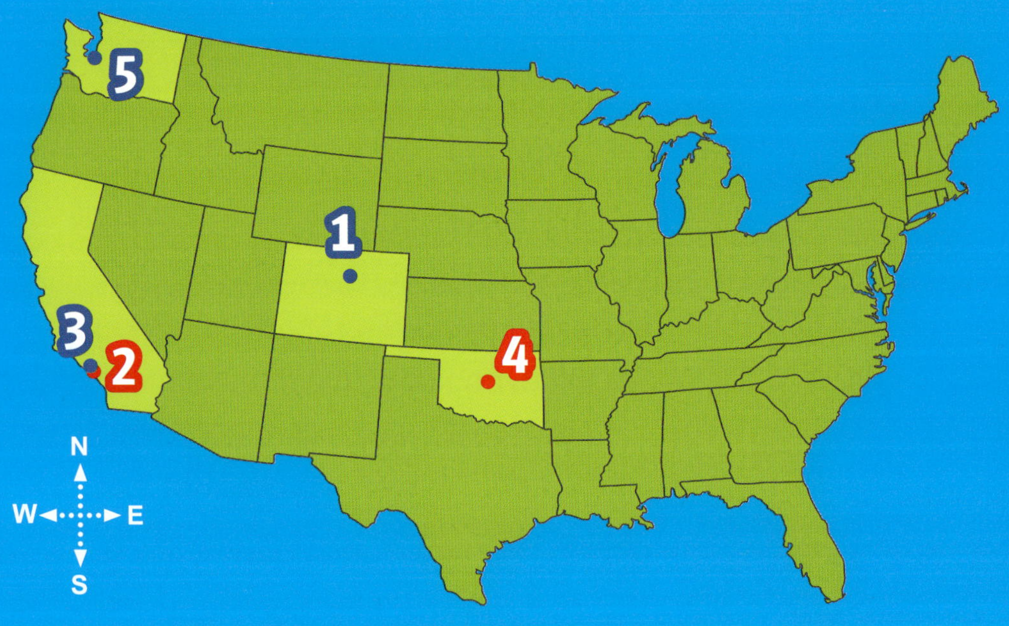

1 **Denver, Colorado:** This is the city where Westbrook set the NBA record for most triple-doubles in one season.

2 **Long Beach, California:** Westbrook was born here on November 12, 1988.

3 **Los Angeles, California:** Westbrook played here for UCLA for two seasons before going to the NBA.

4 **Oklahoma City, Oklahoma:** Westbrook's first season in Oklahoma City was during the 2008–09 season.

5 **Seattle, Washington:** Before moving to Oklahoma City, the Thunder were known as the Seattle SuperSonics. They were the SuperSonics when they drafted Westbrook in 2008.

Russell struggled during his first year there. He averaged only 3.4 points per game. But the UCLA Bruins made it to the **Final Four**.

Russell wanted to be better next year. He woke up at 6:00 a.m. every day in the summer. He worked out and practiced. He played pickup games. Sometimes NBA players like Kobe Bryant joined in.

The hard work paid off. UCLA went back to the Final Four. Russell was named a top defensive player. He decided to leave after his **sophomore** year. It was time to see what he could do in the NBA.

CHAPTER 3

A Family Man

More than 300 kids cheered Russell Westbrook. He handed out high-fives. Then he started handing out presents.

Westbrook was playing Santa. He was hosting a Christmas party for kids. He enjoys meeting Oklahoma City families who need help. During the Christmas season, he brings them clothes and other gifts. He does this as part of his **charity** work. Westbrook has his own charity. It is called the Russell Westbrook Why Not? Foundation.

In December 2017 Westbrook filled up a shopping cart full of toys for kids.

Westbrook started his charity in 2012. He works with kids who face challenges. The charity's name gets people to think about what is possible. Westbrook wants everyone to ask, "Why not?" He wants people to never give up on their dreams. Westbrook's father taught him this lesson.

FUN FACT
Westbrook has one sibling, his younger brother Reynard.

Westbrook also helped open reading centers. He wants kids to read. The NBA gave him an award in 2015 for his charity work.

Westbrook helps his charity serve Thanksgiving dinner to a Los Angeles community in 2016.

Companies hire Westbrook for **endorsements**. He has his own line of basketball shoes. Westbrook enjoys fashion. It is an interest off the court too. In 2013, he signed a deal with an underwear company. He designs custom underwear. He also worked with a fashion company to design jeans. Westbrook has appeared in soda ads too.

Westbrook lives with his wife and children. He met his wife, Nina, at UCLA. She played on the women's basketball team. They married in 2015. Westbrook's oldest child, Noah, was born in 2017. Their twin daughters were born in November 2018.

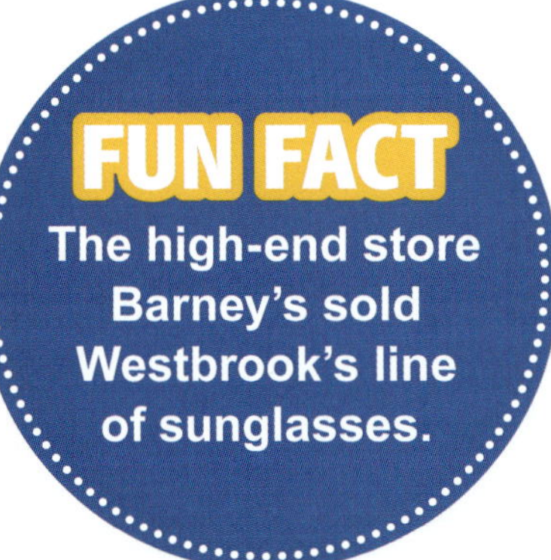

Westbrook enjoys showing off his sense of style.

CAREER TIMELINE

1988

November 12, 1988
Russell Westbrook is born in Long Beach, California.

2007

March 31, 2007
Westbrook plays in the Final Four with UCLA as a freshman.

2008

June 26, 2008
The Seattle SuperSonics select Westbrook with the fourth pick in the NBA Draft.

2008

October 29, 2008
Westbrook makes his NBA debut with the Oklahoma City Thunder.

2012

June 12, 2012
Westbrook plays in his first NBA Finals game with the Thunder.

2017

April 9, 2017
Westbrook sets the NBA record for most triple-doubles in one season.

2017

June 26, 2017
The NBA names Westbrook the 2016–17 Most Valuable Player (MVP).

CHAPTER 4

Thunder and Lightning

Russell Westbrook came into the NBA with Kevin Durant. Together, they turned the Thunder into a great team. Durant and Westbrook played together from 2008 to 2016. Each had his own strengths. Both helped the Thunder win. The team made it to the 2012 NBA Finals.

Durant and Westbrook became successful teammates with the Thunder.

Westbrook could hit any shot. He also wowed fans with dunks. Clips of his dunks became popular online. In 2016, Oklahoma City played the Golden State Warriors in the conference finals. The Thunder went up 3–1 in the series. But the Warriors **rallied** to beat Oklahoma City.

FUN FACT

Westbrook won a gold medal with Team USA at the 2012 Olympics.

ON THE MOVE

The Seattle SuperSonics took Westbrook in the 2008 NBA Draft. He was the fourth pick. Weeks later, things changed. The team moved to Oklahoma City. They became the Thunder. The city of Seattle fought to keep its team. But the owner moved the team anyway. Westbrook played his first season with the Thunder. He never wore a SuperSonics jersey.

Westbrook finished an amazing season in 2017.

Durant became a **free agent** after that season. Many teams wanted him. He decided to go to Golden State. Westbrook stayed in Oklahoma City. He signed a new contract with the Thunder in 2016.

The NBA began in 1949. Until 2017, only one person had averaged a triple-double for a season. Westbrook became the second. He won the Most Valuable Player (MVP) award that season. He beat out other star players such as Stephen Curry and Kawhi Leonard.

Oklahoma City tried to find help for Westbrook. The team traded for Paul George. He was a star for the Indiana Pacers. Westbrook averaged a triple-double again.

FUN FACT

Oscar Robertson was the first NBA player to average a triple-double. He did it in 1962.

Westbrook had another great year in 2018–19. He was close to averaging a triple-double. It came down to the season's last day. Westbrook needed 16 rebounds. He got 20. He got his third triple-double season in a row!

He was already a great player. How great could he be? "He'll go down as a Hall of Famer," George said. "One of the best."

Westbrook continued to shine in 2019.

BEYOND THE BOOK

After reading the book, it's time to think about what you learned. Try the following exercises to jumpstart your ideas.

THINK

THAT'S NEWS TO ME. Russell Westbrook set the NBA record for triple-doubles in a season in 2017. How might news sources be able to fill in more detail about this? What new information could you find in news articles? Where could you go to find those sources?

CREATE

PRIMARY SOURCES. A primary source is an original document, photograph, or interview. Make a list of different primary sources you might be able to find about Westbrook. What new information might you learn from these sources?

SHARE

SUM IT UP. Write one paragraph summarizing the important points from this book. Make sure it's in your own words. Share the paragraph with a classmate. Does your classmate have any comments about the summary? Does he or she have additional questions about Westbrook?

GROW

REAL-LIFE RESEARCH. What places could you visit to learn more about Westbrook? What other things could you learn while you were there?

Visit www.ninjaresearcher.com/0462 to learn how to take your research skills and book report writing to the next level!

RESEARCH

SEARCH LIKE A PRO
Learn about how to use search engines to find useful websites.

FACT OR FAKE?
Discover how you can tell a trusted website from an untrustworthy resource.

TEXT DETECTIVE
Explore how to zero in on the information you need most.

SHOW YOUR WORK
Research responsibly—learn how to cite sources.

WRITE

GET TO THE POINT
Learn how to express your main ideas.

PLAN OF ATTACK
Learn prewriting exercises and create an outline.

DOWNLOADABLE REPORT FORMS

Further Resources

BOOKS

Doeden, Matt. *Russell Westbrook*. Lerner, 2017.

Kortemeier, Todd. *Russell Westbrook: Basketball Star.* Focus Readers, 2018.

Nagelhout, Ryan. *Russell Westbrook: Triple-Double Superstar*. Britannica Educational Publishing, 2019.

WEBSITES

Factsurfer.com gives you a safe, fun way to find more information.

1. Go to www.factsurfer.com.
2. Enter "Russell Westbrook" into the search box and click .
3. Select your book cover to see a list of related websites.

Glossary

assist: When a player passes to another player who then scores a basket, the first player gets an assist. Westbrook got an assist after passing to Kevin Durant.

charity: A charity is a group that helps and raises money for those in need. Westbrook's charity helps kids in Oklahoma City.

endorsements: Endorsements are when someone gives their approval to something. Westbrook does endorsements for products such as soda and clothing.

Final Four: When just four teams are left in the March Madness college basketball tournament, that stage is called the Final Four. UCLA played in the Final Four in 2007.

free agent: A free agent is someone who does not have a contract to play with a team. Kevin Durant became a free agent in 2016.

pickup: In basketball, a pickup game does not have standard officials or rules. Westbrook played a lot of pickup basketball as a kid.

rallied: When a team has overcome a deficit, they have rallied in the game or series. The Golden State Warriors rallied against the Thunder in the 2016 NBA playoffs.

sophomore: A second-year student is called a sophomore. Westbrook was an all-conference player as a sophomore.

triple-doubles: Triple-doubles are recorded when a player has 10 or more of three statistics in a game, such as points or rebounds. Westbrook has gotten triple-doubles in many games.

Index

PHOTO CREDITS

The images in this book are reproduced through the courtesy of: Brian Rothmuller/Icon Sportswire/AP Images, front cover (center), p. 9 (Russell Westbrook); Sue Ogrocki/AP Images, front cover (right), pp. 3, 6–7, 16–17; David Zalubowski/AP Images, pp. 4–5; Ververidis Vasilis/Shutterstock Images, p. 7; Jack Dempsey/AP Images, p. 8; Red Line Editorial, pp. 9 (chart), 14; Daniel Loncarevic/Shutterstock Images, pp. 10, 21 (top); asife/Shutterstock Images, pp. 10–11; Christian Petersen/Getty Images Sport/Getty Images, pp. 12–13; Photo Works/Shutterstock, p. 15; s_bukley/Shutterstock Images, p. 16; Lilly Lawrence/Getty Images Entertainment/Getty Images, pp. 18–19; Featureflash Photo Agency/Shutterstock Images, p. 20; Lightspring/Shutterstock Images, p. 21 (bottom); Jeff Roberson/AP Images, p. 22; Victor Maschek/Shutterstock Images, p. 24; David J. Phillip/AP Images, pp. 24–25; Oleksiy Naumov/Shutterstock Images, p. 26; Brandon Dill/AP Images, pp. 26–27; Cressida Studio/Shutterstock Images, p. 30.

ABOUT THE AUTHOR

Kevin Frederickson is a freelance writer and editor from Ohio. He lives near Cincinnati with his golden doodle, Max.